in case of emergency press

We are proud to acknowledge the Traditional Owners of country throughout Australia and to recognise their continuing connection to land, waters, and culture. We pay our respects to their Elders.

We support recognition, reconciliation, and reparation.

Learning to Love in Winter

Angelo J. Letizia

in case of emergency press
https://icoe.com.au
Travancore, Victoria
Australia

Published by in case of emergency press 2024

Copyright © Angelo J. Letizia 2024

All rights reserved. Without limiting the rights under copyright reserved above, no part of this publication may be reproduced, stored in or introduced into a database and retrieval system or transmitted in any form or any means (electronic, mechanical, photocopying, recording or otherwise) without the prior written permission of both the owner of copyright and the above publishers.

ISBN: 978-0-6486111-0-3

Cover design: Ward Nikriph

Cover photograph: Кристина Фатина on Unsplash

Acknowledgements

I would like to acknowledge all the help I have had along the way.

Dedication

For TRL, RRL and CBL

Table of Contents

Preface v

Learning to Love in Winter 1
Rape the land 2
The Stuff of Life 3
Enjoying the Name 4
This is all wrong 5
Hammers 6
The New Prayer 7
There is no punctuation in the sun 8
Where are the patterns? 9
Boredom Leads to Evil 10
The Gifts 11
Death by Fire at a Youth Field Hockey Game 12
I wonder 13
Ingredients 14
Ataxia 15
We are drawn to what kills us 16
5:15 am 17
I don't want your awards 18
The Cave 19
I cannot 20
Ghost of Enlightenment 22
The Yellow Books 23
The Fire Inside 24
When the time comes 25
Recycle the stars 26
Partition the signs 27
Loadbearing Cell 28
With My Daughter 29
Accountability 30
Live in the debris 31

Heroes	32
Driving on a Maryland Highway	33
I waited for Jesus	34
The hidden places	35
There are so many universes I did not even know about	36
Gone	37
Porch Philosophy	38
I am sick of pop stars and athletes	39
Somewhere	40
Livestream	41
On the Nature Trail I had a Revelation of Sorts	42
Heidegger would not be proud	43
All our formulas	44
I wandered in the forest	45
Where will we live?	46
Never mind	47
I have grown tired	48
Syntax	49
Invent the grass each minute	50
Network	51
Exponential	52
Divinity	53
Dividing Space	54
We must lay the stones	55
They are still here?	56
Hospital poem	57
About the Author	61

Learning to Love in Winter

Angelo J. Letizia

Preface

Where I come from, the Northeastern United States, winter is usually hard and bleak. The days are short and mostly sunless. When it snows, the roads freeze and make travel hazardous, and when the snow does thaw some, there is a mess of gravel, slush and trash. This, to me, always represented a sort of bleak, gray oblivion, hidden in plain sight. I realize this is not everyone's experience, especially people who live in warmer or different climates, but perhaps a similar feeling might be felt in the desert or a polluted city. Wherever we are, this oblivion awaits, patiently, inexorably, to swallow everything we know. And perhaps I glimpsed it unwittingly on some random winter day in the Northern Hemisphere.

If there is some oblivion waiting, what should we do? I guess we should try to build something, to love each other, to create, experience and teach, to learn. Perhaps we have to learn to love in the winter, or in the desert or whatever time and place you feel the yawning oblivion beginning to swallow you, perhaps it's while you are eating your cereal or driving home from work on a sunny day.

But why? I don't know. Maybe loving is a way to mitigate oblivion, at least temporarily. Maybe we should give up and succumb to it, die in the snow or the desert—this would be much easier. It gets harder every day to build and to love. But I think we have to keep trying, perhaps out of instinct, habit, conditioning or simply because there is nothing else to do.

Each poem in this book represents an attempt to love or build or teach in the snow, in that trash-filled and quiet void. Each poem is an attempt to expose the snow, but, if that is how the poems will be judged, then most of the poems in this book are probably failures because many of them succumb to oblivion. But maybe, even a failure is progress here, in the snow.

Angelo J. Letizia
Manchester, MD
October 2023

Learning to Love in Winter

We must learn
To love in Winter
Learn to love in the black snow
Trampled underfoot by hard boots
Love under the hard sky
And salted streets
Have faith the roots
Are still under
The frozen ground
We must learn to love
Without words or sunlight
Embrace the snow
And draw strength from its sad granules
There is no salvation in the snow
And we should love it for that

Rape the land

With mile markers and state lines
Rape the darkness
With light
I am the universe
Thinking of itself
Thinking of bad thoughts
I am the universe's
Artificial vision
The universe cannot see in the dark
Without light
And I love all
These plastic things
The maps are paper sepulchers
Ossified remnants
Of blood
Which cakes on the flue
I turn west
And bend the light
I see Kansas
And around the globe
And back to the westward-turned head
I only see here
In this desert

The Stuff of Life

Gasoline and hand soap
Are made from the same stuff
Fuel, cleanliness, all the important things
Use Neosporin to heal a star
The mirrors have grown tails
Paint the bleach
And offer a libation
To all your memories
To the rocks that surrounded your childhood home
Sacrifice every condom
To every child that could have been
To the gods you no longer believe in
And pray for the sun to accelerate its pace
And swallow the earth
A billion years sooner

Enjoying the Name

I don't have any more dreams or desires
I don't even have thoughts really
Just residue, soot in an oil furnace
Maybe this is a natural process of loss
Of losing your name
I wanted to give it back anyway
And be a temporary collection of atoms
While others win awards
And live normal lives
I wanted to wait for the dissolution
Into corners and paint
Maybe then
I can finally enjoy the name
In some indirect way

This is all wrong

The source is dead
Universes and cancer
Metastasize
but they are the only
Places to live now
In the visions
In the trash
Where we marry
And the cold jelly
Of the stars
Drips
In our mouths
When we pray
When we create our gods
This is all wrong though
But we don't know any better

Hammers

There was no motive
For the act
So, I must accept
All that hurts
There is no should
Only ink and gasoline
Only breeze and cancer
In the stars and
Hammers fall from the moon
So, nothing can be built
Truth, cells pavement
All look the same now
Like primordial soup
Which bubbles in my cereal where
Cornflakes should be
The taste of things
Is oddly familiar
Warm, like a woman
Reverse abortion
Push the universe back into the womb
And try again

The New Prayer

I must accept the death of a sun
Accept the hue of the grass
And the end of lovers
Abandoned and vacant houses bloom
In the objectivity
There is data for all this
Locked somewhere in the grammar of the universe
Or in the DNA of a microbe
Long extinct
But it lived long enough
To ensure
That I would suffer

There is no punctuation in the sun

There is no punctuation in the sun
No commas in the tree bark
There is only the darkness of the apple kidney
And a cancer made of hardwood
Abandon logic
To the humidity
Abandon all your cells
To infinity
Drown the water
In snow and light
Live in the desert of all things

Where are the patterns?

Where are the patterns?
Where are the voices?
Perhaps they are flattened
Into dusty and noiseless things

But

I got bored with this evolution
With its patterns
So I changed my blood
Into a star
Changed my heart
Into a new grammar

That you cannot understand

Boredom Leads to Evil

I got bored with life
But dying was too much work
So, I decided to transform
I turned my blood into the sky
Let it drop in your cereal
I turned my heart
Into gasoline and
My feet
Into vegetable oil
I fashioned my spine into a ghost
To haunt your ex-lovers
And finally
I made my brain
Evolve into a new galaxy
Of rocks and ice
Where I could live alone

The Gifts

What gifts have you given me?
Paint, anxiety and turpentine?
Each tooth transformed into a star
Lined with regret
But the light does not reach
Not yet at least
Oh
But the starlight methodically creeps through the vacuum
Like a pestilence
Like a pack of nomads wandering to find new herds
All their clay pots rattle

Death by Fire at a Youth Field Hockey Game

Holocausts slumber in paint
Only to assist the gate

Which opens to the last dream

Enjamb the yield curve
With broken concrete

Stitch the net

Over anything you can
Watch the fish die

Do you still think you are a fisher of men?

I wonder

I wonder if there are
Doors in the sun where
Gasoline
And helium sweat
On the impossible wooden
frames

I wonder if there
are tunnels in the outer
Core where dreams drop from the
Mantle like a
Garbage chute

What else is
Hidden in the hospitals and
The salt
Mines deep under
The cold earth?

Ingredients

Olive oil, pepper and
A can of crushed tomatoes
Black coffee, liquor
And twine, red paint and chlorine
Transform themselves
Into the atoms of the world
Nuclei of an unholy union
Which I am crucified on daily
Each couch is my Golgotha

Ataxia

The plastic jars
Warp in the sun
Yellow lids
Give up the secret
Of their ataxia
Unstable plastic
Wobbling in the air
Cremate your sovereignty
And every other idea
That gives you comfort
Let them all break
Let them all die
Melt the constricting plastic
To a puddle
And see the sun
For the first time

We are drawn to what kills us

Maybe the thing
We are trying to save
Is actually killing us
Maybe
It's a liminal phase
Not one thing
Or the other
Maybe its a type of birth
Which doubles as a death
But only the noble parts die
In succession
We get to watch
Maybe we should let them die
And live in the embers
There is certain
Wisdom in the ashes

5:15 AM

The sunrise is no oracle
But there may be wisdom in it yet
Birds and stars swim in the burgeoning light
I knew things once
But the light is like cancer
Now I just listen to birds
Mistakes and coffee drop peacefully
And the trees are a fortress
Where I can rationalize my desires
There are no people before dawn
And even the concrete seems natural
At least for a while

I don't want your awards

I don't want your awards
I don't want your awards
Anymore
I don't want the rain
But used too
I don't want your praise
Or your extrinsic grace
Just give me
A garden
And some books
Let me grow old
And watch the world change
Into something
Unrecognizable
I don't want your awards

The Cave

There might be
Two things in everything
What we see
And what is there
Or perhaps
Some intersubjective mean
Which pours over
Like tar
In a college syllabus

I cannot

I cannot build a deck
Or repair the starter
In your old car
I didn't find the septic tank
Because I cannot drive a backhoe
I didn't frame the basement
"Did you do this? Did you use power tools?"
"Yes" I said with a smile
And with oven mitts on
But the railing I built is ugly and so is the shed
You are much smarter than me
Even though I went to college
And have multiple degrees
I am not brave and I don't sleep in tents
I don't use guns
I don't defend schools or shopping malls
I sit at a desk and read Plato (in English)
And my poems do not sell
You could never have married me
Because I can't drive a tractor
And repair ball bearings
I didn't invent a water brick
To absorb moisture
I am not a self made millionaire
I don't have a house in Tobago
And I don't own a bank
My achievements are small
And fleeting
When I die

Learning to Love in Winter

My children will forget me
As they work their normal jobs
But
I am memory
And I fuel the universe as it dies
I am the fuel of death

Ghost of Enlightenment

Ghost of Enlightenment
Crucify your martyrs
Give up your teleological innards
Nail them to the wood too
A forest of crosses to atone
For the holocausts
But we have grown tired of trying to atone
There is no one to atone to
Except the rain which is the only god left now
The plastic and paint and steel doors
Have rejected logic
And figured out how to live
They terrorize me at night
When I make love to my wife
When I wait
For my son in the rain in my old car
I am scared of the water
And all the broken pieces of utopia
That I call my home

The Yellow Books

The yellow books are plotting their
Revenge
The dead philosophers and
Farmers
Are tired
Of budgets
Paint has spilled
Into the stars again
And the stars
Are now
Containers hung in
The sky
Each brick has a mouth and tongue
Like you
Each brick
Swallows all the trees
Like you
But you cannot hold it all
So you vomit
All the bricks and guitars
All the paint and salt and baseballs
You vomit it all up
Because it's immoral

The Fire Inside

A fire has consumed all the ventricles
And each lamp becomes
A new world
Shine and spoken
Pepper and surgeons
Spread the ash
You could understand this
With a level of consciousness
With breasts that nourish

When the time comes

When the time comes
Your heroes will all be exposed as charlatans
When the time comes
Your entrepreneurs will be exposed as swindlers
When the time comes
The silent and forgotten will take the throne
When the time comes
You will know

Recycle the stars

Recycle the stars
Into garbage
And perform surgery
On the snow
Cold sterile
Hospital is
A manifestation of logic
The inverted joke
Which you are forbidden to laugh at
The rubber and linoleum
Might have souls

Partition the signs

Partition the signs
So they can read
The cartography of sanity
Blooms in the paint
Japanese Maple is a
Phoneme which portends
Meaning
Dirt and chlorine
Are atoms
At least temporarily

Loadbearing Cell

Humidity has broken
The support
The aging skeleton of the houses
And forms
The archetype is rendered
Obsolete
The sun cannot stand
And neither can the apple tree
With the withered bark
All the bricks and fire pits
Crumble into a undifferentiated mass
Baptize the rubble make it
A eucharist
Baptize the sinners
And watch them wander in the forest
Because your baptism is only a ceremony
Light and noise and bread
Distilled to salt and honey
To spread on the mountains

With My Daughter

For one afternoon
I have become the soul
Of the Catoctin Mountains
I am the breeze and I move through
Your oaks
The furnaces pump
Their black soot too
The vistas and leaves are underfoot
The maples and the shade
I become its blood
And as I return to the pathway
I realize the purpose
For all of this, the purpose
For the universe
Is this rock
That I sit on, with my daughter

Accountability

Are false suns accountable
To all the things they burn?
The wood they rot and the colors they fade?
What makes a god?
Gasoline? Cadmium? Electronic light?
Made up gods are not accountable to anyone
Except to the poets

Live in the debris

I am tired of
Creating suns in my basement
No one appreciates these masterpieces anymore
Yellow consciousness and helium
Will rise to a different galaxy now
I am shutting down the old machines
Their rusty gears
Are tired and can sleep
I will never ask them to produce another star
Or compass
The old doors are all humanity has left now
Because I won't make any more of these
No one cares about ice, humidity, trees, seeds, iron or sand
I won't make any of these things either
I am closing the factory
Let the primates wander in their beautiful obsolescence
Of the things they can no longer replace

Heroes

we crucified you
2000 years ago
Robespierre and Nietzsche tried to kill you too
but I still see you sometimes
smoking cigarettes
walking alone at night,
it's a sad thing
to watch a god
who doesn't know when to die

Driving on a Maryland Highway

plant killers in soil
cultivate them as citizens
drown saints in red paint
and coat all the crucifixes
in rubber
build utopia
with cadmium and magnesium
and bury me
in rain water

I waited for Jesus

I waited for Jesus
to pop the nails from his hands and feet
and come down off the wood and
walk across the desert
I waited for him in my kitchen
I opened a bottle of wine
but he never came
so I drank alone
I imagined his bloody feet caked with mud
tracking sand everywhere
I imagined how I would talk to him
unload my burdens
and how he would listen
but he never showed
so I just got drunk and fell asleep

The hidden places

The hidden places
ooze in the wooden planks
drip slowly in the summer
we live in these spaces
in the life between
the hammer and blood
there is an ocean
and a geography
which explodes
there is a wheelchair
which gets used to traverse new worlds
dwarf planets
rotate into the sun
that no one calls a sun
but I will know

There are so many universes I did not even know about

Each tooth is a universe
A trapdoor in the jaw
An entrance to a memory
Which breaks on the shore
Of a dream
We wander through the forest now
Alone, scared, without Enlightenment
But we are better off without it
We always were
There are doors everywhere
If you know where to look
But there are still no saviors

Gone

The sun
Has broken
Its skeleton
Brittle arm bone
Covered in gasoline
Fold the galaxy
Into a poem
Measure the negative space
Make meaning from ice
And from the light years

Porch Philosophy

We sat on your porch
In North Carolina
We drank beer
And looked at the stars
I told you
The light takes billions of years
To reach the earth
But the star is dead
This was before our marriage
Before kids and the PhD
Before I thought I knew everything
But the light is still trying to come to earth
And the star is still dead

I am sick of pop stars and athletes

Bitter universes
shrivel
As you eat your noodles
I smell the snow
And I pray to the god
I created
It stands in the water
In Mexico
It begs for heads and blood
And receipts
And all the things of modern life
But the boxes are empty
So I can kill them with killers
Because there is no difference
Between killers and saviors

Somewhere

There is a nail
Somewhere in India
Or South Sudan
It holds two pieces of
Rotting wood together

Two forgotten fragments of the universe
Buried deep in an abandoned house

Two pieces of infrastructure
That the universe could not live without

Perhaps this rusty nail
Is some sort of linchpin
Which keeps the universe functioning
Keeps it working

For now

Livestream

I saw my death advertised
And my birth livestreamed
But I still have no savior
So I found a referent hiding
In the pantry
So I crucified it
On a plastic cross
But it didn't work
The crucifixion was a joke
I was still purposeless
Even though I was promised
I would be saved

On the Nature Trail I had a Revelation of Sorts

Purple evenings
And sugary afternoons
Lap upon a distant shore
Where radiance is bartered for berries
With hominids
All of whom
Had more potential
Than you ever did
Those beings could have foretold
The meaning
Of the green cotton sunlight
On a painted barn
While you count your invoices
Or paint your home

Heidegger would not be proud

Being is a type of truth
And so is art
A black priestess boils rinds
In a dark hut
This is truth, too
Salted meat
Broken keyboards
Form some grotesque
Hieroglyph
Which twists into meaning
Alongside the bulbous pears

All our formulas

All our formulas
Led us to this
It's a wilderness
But not the one we thought
A broken piston
And pharmaceutical degrees
Yawn in the democracy
Of our oblivion
We cannot legislate
The fear
At the end of this Enlightenment
Because it led to a dumpster
We had to pay for it
Without doubt and with
Feigned certainties

I wandered in the forest

I wandered in the forest
And knew it was right
The formulas and numbers
Became useless
Swirling in the dead leaves
There was beauty in it
Beauty in the stillness when
They came to rest
Beauty in the notion that
what once had power to control
Withers on the forest floor

Where will we live?

I wonder where we will live
When it's over
When the primates decide
To finally push that button
I wonder what will be left
What will be used for currency
I wonder if we will learn
That it could have been
So much better

Never mind

I don't know
If it makes sense
To start this
So close to the end
The stage hands
Are packing up the props
And the flag is folded
The audience is leaving
And has lost interest
The set director
Is smoking a cigarette outside
And the ashes slowly, inexorably
Drop to the concrete

I have grown tired

I have grown tired
Of the present arrangement
Of these deceptive atoms
Which give the illusion of truth
And the shadows that cling
To them for warmth
These things limit
What I can think
Atoms and shadows
Spawn a restrictive grammar
Which crowns itself as objective
But I have no such consent
An autocracy of feeling
And forgetting
That was always something more

Syntax

I invented a new language with
Signifiers of teeth and arteries
And the saddest referents
Which are more accurate
Than the old meaningless words
They were just echoes of nothing
Guttural sounds clanging in the void
Now, blood runs between signifier and referent
And infinity throbs
Dripping over stars
Filling mop buckets and shot glasses
A new grammar of light
Settling in this reborn universe
We will have to relearn everything

Invent the grass each minute

Invent the grass each minute
Construct the sky and walls
Build the floor
Before you walk on it
Dream the air
And imagine your sorrow
Its all there
Every moment
Replicating itself
With pain and steel and electricity
Throbbing in the brain
Pulsating in the idea
That existed before
Any human thought it

Network

I see the connections
Which ripen in the simulacra
Blossoming into questions
With no tongues to speak them
And no brains to process
A breast and cool breeze
Elaborate sunshine
In a memory
The hill between hearts
And a broken rind
Which leaks from the sun
All these things
Somehow become the answer
I need

Exponential

There are connections
Between pieces
Between name and thing
Links that yawn back into
The first thought
But things exist in space
Things throb in the emptiness
Which they draw strength from
A billion heart like structures
Power this universe
And the thought of the next
These celestial batteries
Undercut the supposed busyness
And the comings and goings
Of important men
Who die anyway

Divinity

When you died
Did your ghost
Just sit in the empty church
Waiting to be saved?
You quickly learned
Augustine was wrong
The world is not god's speech
But her excrement
Shit in the clouds
Shit in the mouth
Thales said gods are in everything
Maybe in the rim and tongue
Holy things
We pray to
But the tabernacle
Participates in a different way
The metal is a restraint,
A division of the good
And the collection basket
He is still waiting
In the church, decades later
And god is still not there

Dividing Space

I participate in the division
By thinking about a lake
And smoking a cigarette
The gods used to be in everything
They left now
And I sit alone
There are no gods and we have to save ourselves
We become batteries
To power and birth a
Million new ideas
To sustain us in an empty department store
As we slowly transform
Into a beginning

We must lay the stones

We must lay the stones
And bring the shovels
We must participate
Paint the fences
And lay the corners
Between the things
That most do not notice
We must build
The invisible infrastructure
And give it a name
And then
Watch it usurp
Everything they love

They are still here?

I see them
Sometimes
Smoking cigarettes as they
Mutter old party slogans
Bosses with no one to lead
All the forgotten rallies
Boxes of pamphlets and old books
Where are you now?
Your ideas were wrong
Wrong theories, wrong formulations
Lost forgotten
Judged inadequate
What did you leave us?
Except maybe a joke
Or antithesis to be overcome

Hospital poem

There is still something left
It's insidious
Like the sunrise
Which you expected
Which you hoped for
Which you prayed for
But I prayed to a dead star
To a husk
Hung up in the sky
And I wagered that husk
Against a universe
That a little boy
Would not die
On the clean linen sheets

About the Author

Angelo J. Letizia is a professor of education at Notre Dame of Maryland University in Baltimore, Maryland.

In addition to *Learning to Love in Winter*, Angelo has published *Toward the Real* with **in case of emergency press**.

He has also published four books of poetry with **Silver Bow Press**, and numerous academic monographs, articles, and essays.

He lives in the United States of America with his wife and three children.